ABOUT KUMON

KUMON®
MATH. READING. SUCCESS.

What is Kumon?

Kumon is the world's largest supplemental education provider and a leader in producing outstanding results. After-school programs in math and reading at Kumon Centers around the globe have been helping children succeed for 50 years.

Kumon Workbooks represent just a fraction of our complete curriculum of preschool-to-college-level material assigned at Kumon Centers under the supervision of trained Kumon Instructors.

The Kumon Method enables each child to progress successfully by practicing material until concepts are mastered and advancing in small, manageable increments. Instructors carefully assign materials and pace advancement according to the strengths and needs of each individual student.

Students usually attend a Kumon Center twice a week and practice at home the other five days. Assignments take about twenty minutes.

Kumon helps students of all ages and abilities master the basics, improve concentration and study habits, and build confidence.

How did Kumon begin?

IT ALL BEGAN IN JAPAN 50 YEARS AGO when a parent and teacher named Toru Kumon found a way to help his son Takeshi do better in school. At the prompting of his wife, he created a series of short assignments that his son could complete successfully in less than 20 minutes a day and that would ultimately make high school math easy. Because each was just a bit more challenging than the last, Takeshi was able to master the skills and gain the confidence to keep advancing.

This unique self-learning method was so successful that Toru's son was able to do calculus by the time he was in the sixth grade. Understanding the value of good reading comprehension, Mr. Kumon then developed a reading program employing the same method. His programs are the basis and inspiration of those offered at Kumon Centers today under the expert guidance of professional Kumon Instructors.

Mr. Toru Kumon
Founder of Kumon

What can Kumon do for my child?

Kumon is geared to children of all ages and skill levels. Whether you want to give your child a leg up in his or her schooling, build a strong foundation for future studies or address a possible learning problem, Kumon provides an effective program for developing key learning skills given the strengths and needs of each individual child.

What makes Kumon so different?

Kumon uses neither a classroom model nor a tutoring approach. It's designed to facilitate self-acquisition of the skills and study habits needed to improve academic performance. This empowers children to succeed on their own, giving them a sense of accomplishment that fosters further achievement. Whether for remedial work or enrichment, a child advances according to individual ability and initiative to reach his or her full potential. Kumon is not only effective, but also surprisingly affordable.

What is the role of the Kumon Instructor?

Kumon Instructors regard themselves more as mentors or coaches than teachers in the traditional sense. Their principal role is to provide the direction, support and encouragement that will guide the student to performing at 100% of his or her potential. Along with their rigorous training in the Kumon Method, all Kumon Instructors share a passion for education and an earnest desire to help children succeed.

KUMON FOSTERS:

- A mastery of the basics of reading and math
- Improved concentration and study habits
- Increased self-discipline and self-confidence
- A proficiency in material at every level
- Performance to each student's full potential
- A sense of accomplishment

▶▶ GETTING STARTED IS EASY. Just call us at 877.586.6671 or visit kumon.com to request our free brochure and find a Kumon Center near you. We'll direct you to an Instructor who will be happy to speak with you about how Kumon can address your child's particular needs and arrange a free placement test. There are more than 1,700 Kumon Centers in the U.S. and Canada, and students may enroll at any time throughout the year, even summer. Contact us today.

FIND OUT MORE ABOUT KUMON MATH & READING CENTERS.
Receive a free copy of our parent guide, *Every Child an Achiever,* by visiting kumon.com/go.survey or calling 877.586.6671

1 Counting 1 to 10

To parents

Write your child's name and the date in the boxes above. First, make sure that your child can count from 1 to 10. When your child completes each exercise, praise him or her.

■ Draw a line from 1 to 10 in order while saying each number.

■Draw a line from 1 to 10 in order while saying each number.

2 Writing Numbers 1 to 10

Name

Date

To parents
Have your child say the numbers aloud while doing the exercise. Is he or she able to write from 1 to 10 easily?

■Trace the gray numeral in each crayon. Next, trace the dotted numeral. Write the numeral in the bottom box. Say the number aloud.

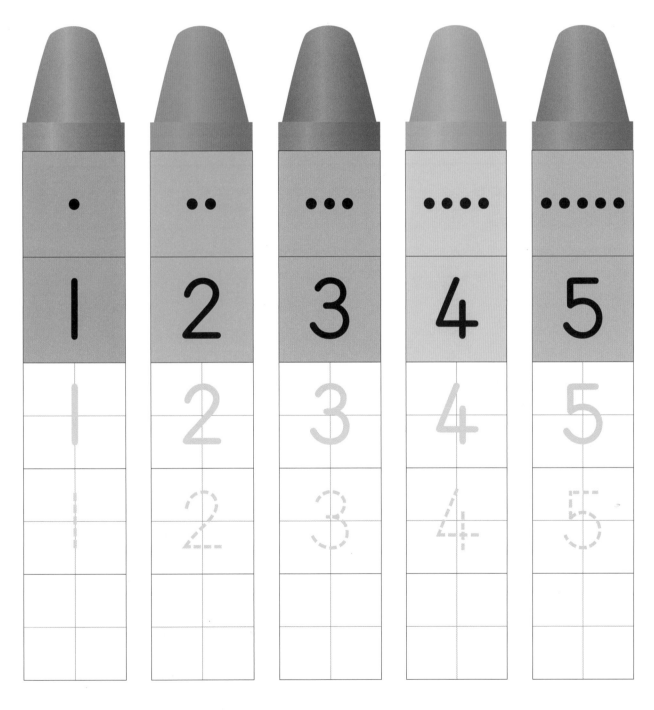

■Trace the gray numeral in each crayon. Next, trace the dotted numeral. Write the numeral in the bottom box. Say the number aloud.

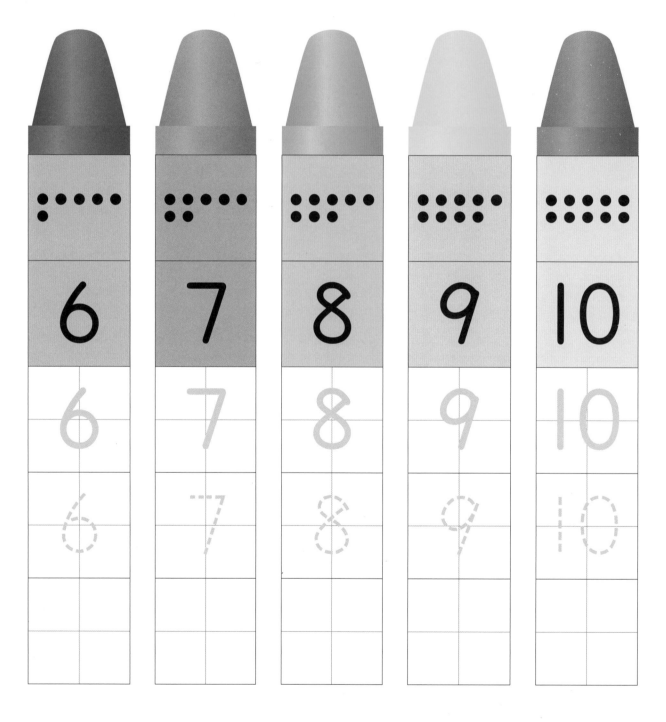

Writing Numbers 1 to 10

To parents
In addition to being a sequence, numbers also represent quantities. Have your child count the dot(s) (●) while doing the exercise. It is important for your child to practice counting in daily activities.

■How many dots (●) are there? Trace the gray numbers.

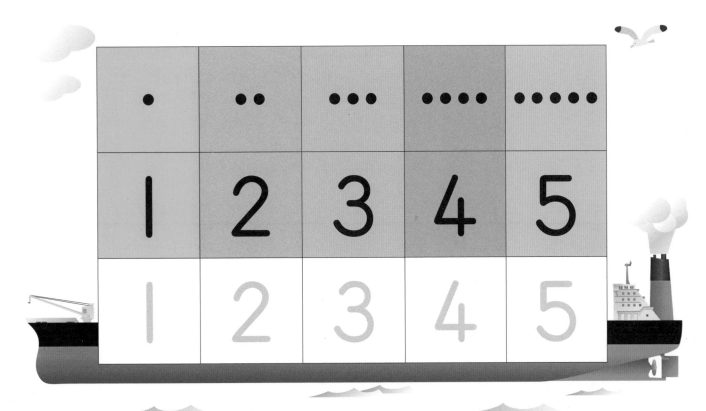

■How many dots (●) are there?
 Trace the gray numbers and fill in the empty boxes.

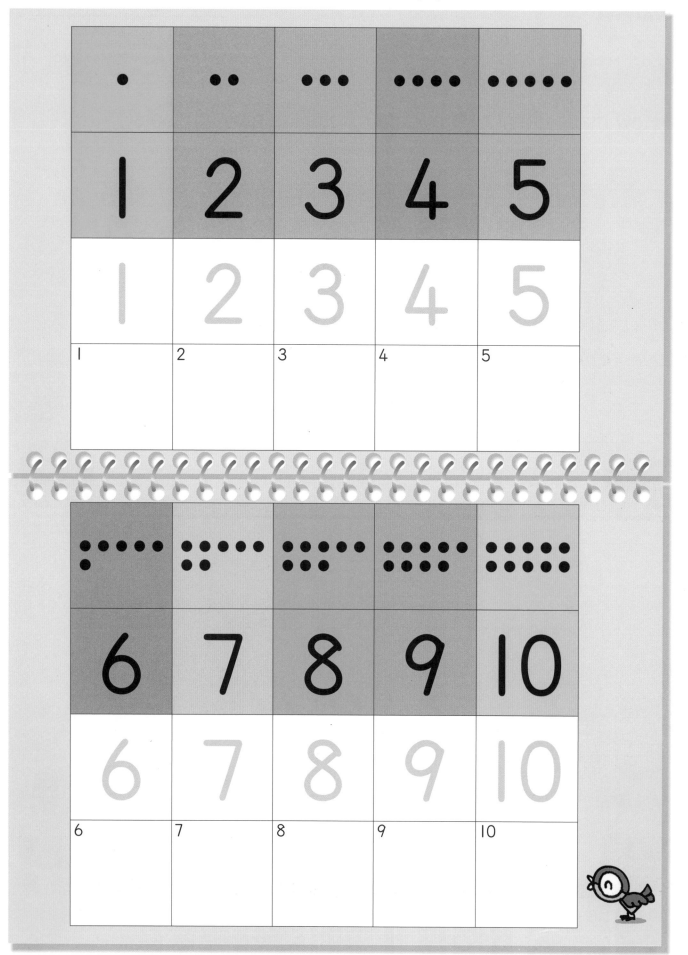

4 Number Puzzle 1 to 20
Giraffe Goes for a Drive

Name

Date

To parents

Have your child learn the order of the numbers from 1 to 20. Lines might be shaky at first, but when your child completes the exercise, praise him or her.

■ Draw a line from 1 to 20 in order while saying each number.

Catching a Butterfly

■Draw a line from 1 to 20 in order while saying each number.

5 Writing Numbers 11 to 20

Name

Date

■Trace the gray numeral in each crayon. Next, trace the dotted numeral. Write the numeral in the bottom box. Say the number aloud.

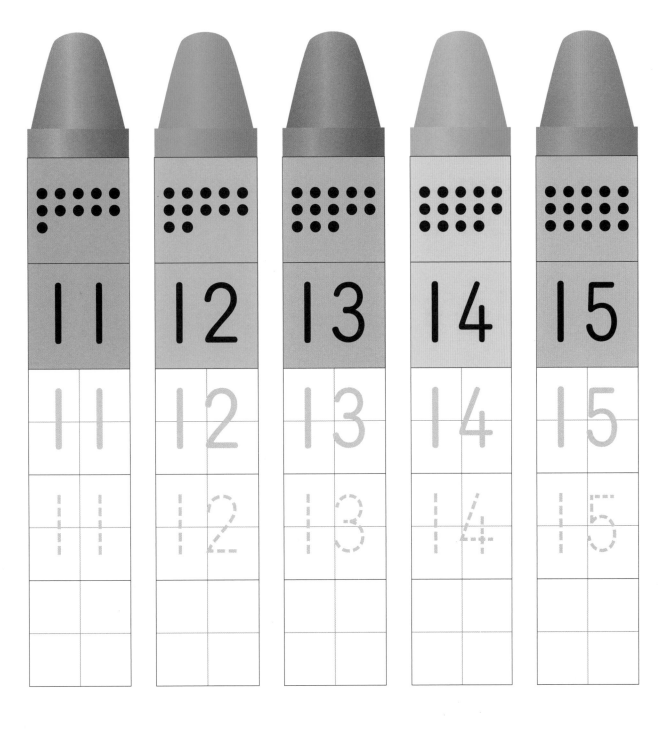

■Trace the gray numeral in each crayon. Next, trace the dotted numeral. Write the numeral in the bottom box. Say the number aloud.

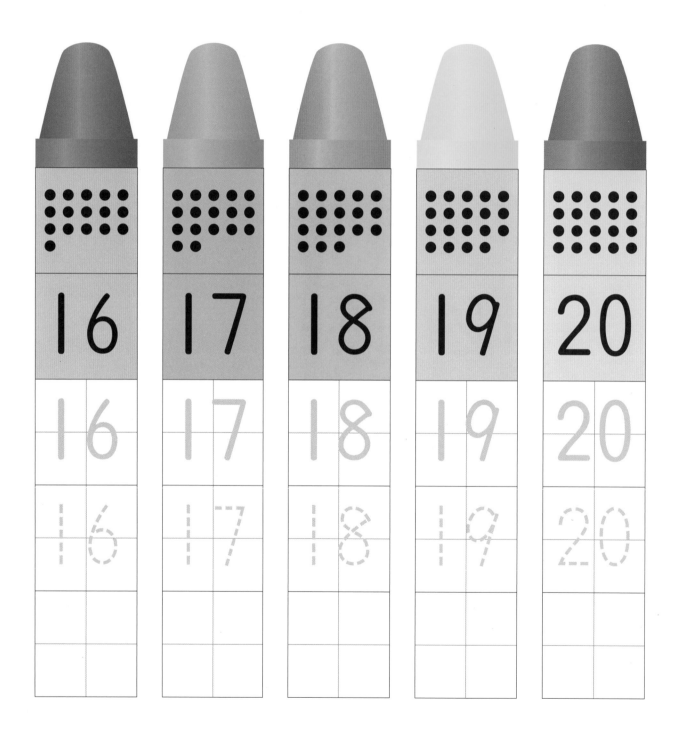

■How many dots (●) are there? Trace the gray numbers.

■How many dots (●) are there?
Trace the gray numbers and fill in the empty boxes.

Name	
Date	

To parents
When your child is able to write the numbers well, praise him or her.

■ Trace the gray numbers. Then fill in the missing numbers.
Say each number aloud.

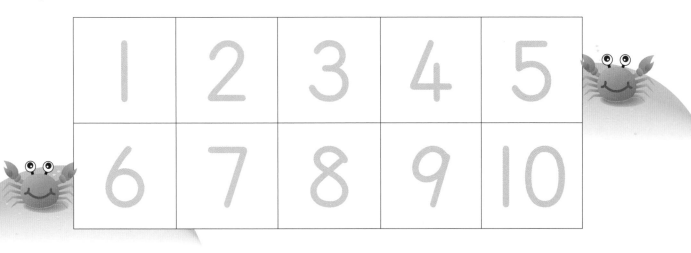

■ Trace the gray numbers. Then fill in the missing numbers. Say each number aloud.

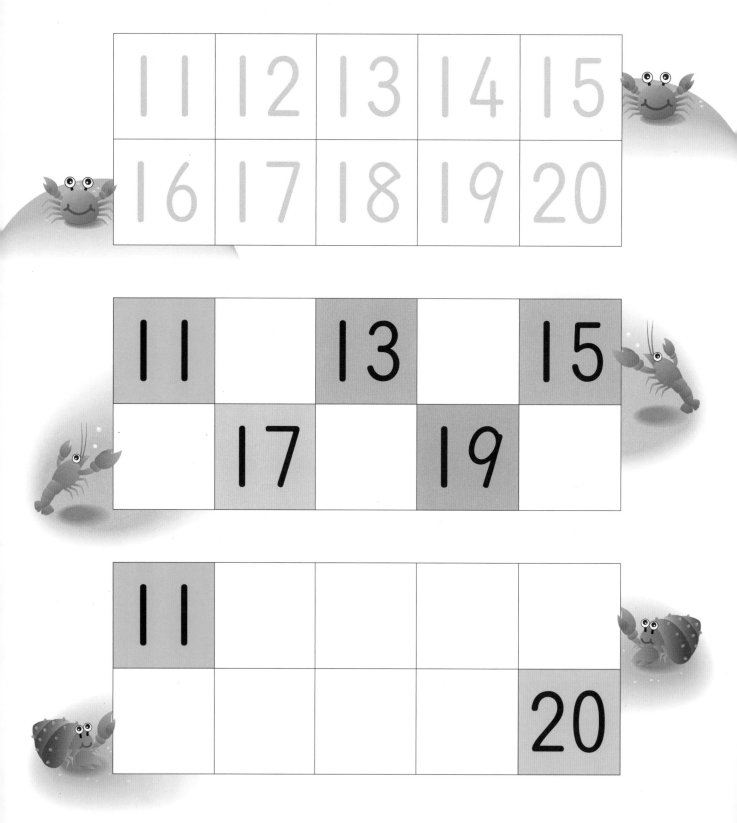

8 Numbers 1 to 20

Name

Date

■ Fill in the missing numbers. Say each number aloud.

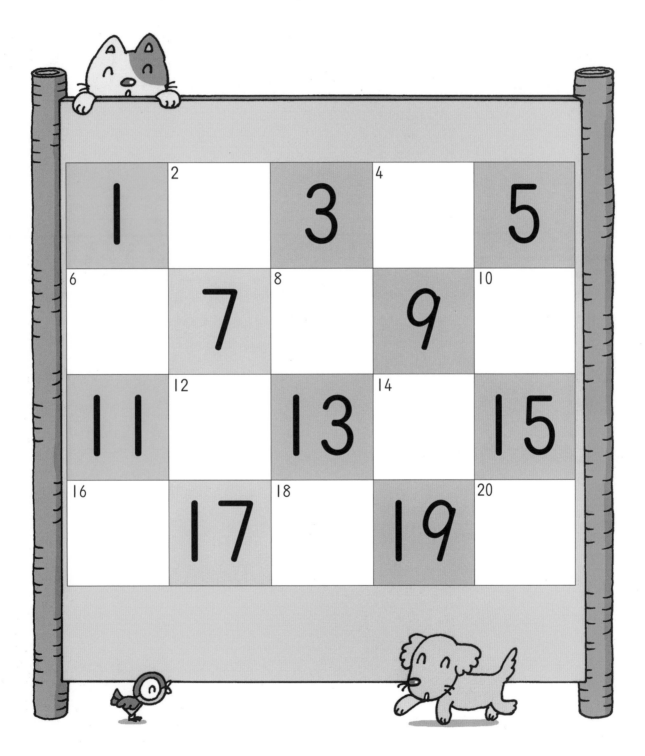

■ Fill in the missing numbers. Say each number aloud.

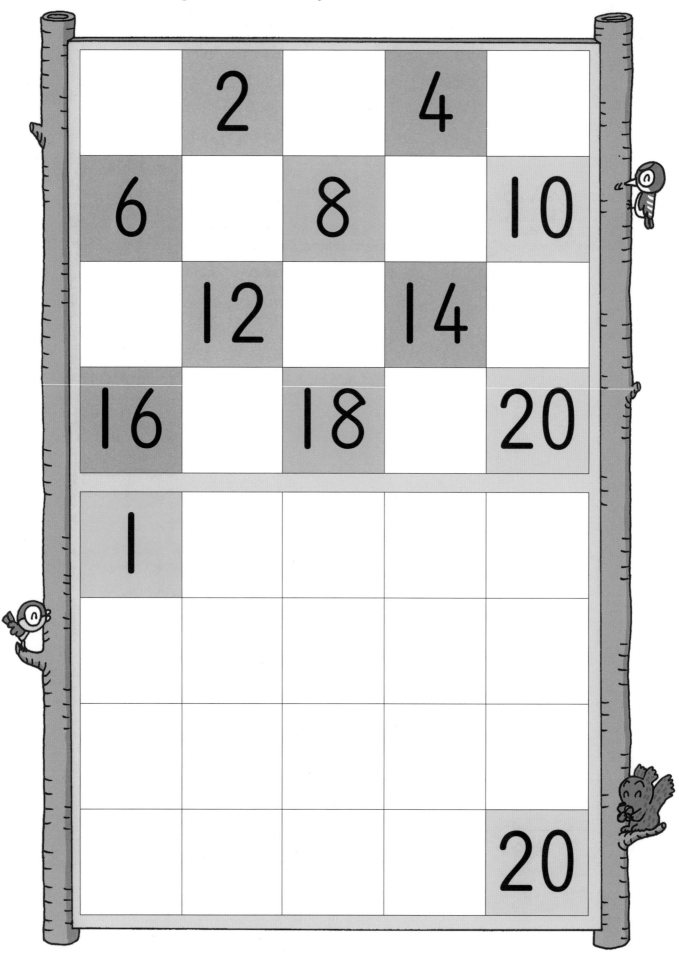

	2		4	
6		8		10
	12		14	
16		18		20

1				
				20

Number Puzzle 1 to 30
Steam Engine

Name

Date

■Draw a line from 1 to 30 in order while saying each number.

Balloon Friends

Number Puzzle 1 to 30
Baboon

Name

Date

■Draw a line from 1 to 30 in order while saying each number.

What Is Under the Ground?

■Draw a line from 1 to 30 in order while saying each number.

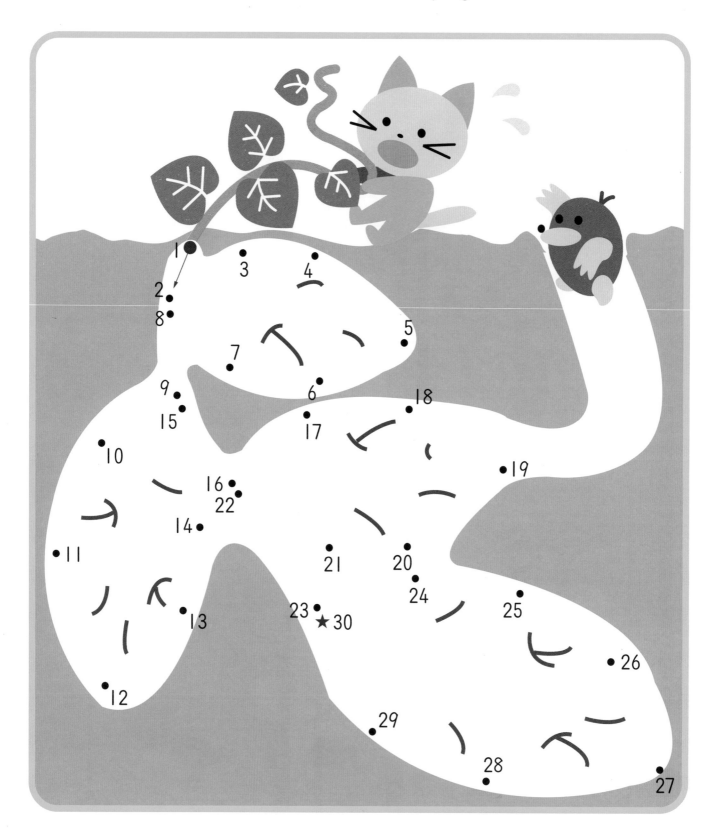

Writing Numbers
21 to 30

■Trace the gray numbers and fill in the empty boxes.
 Say each number aloud.

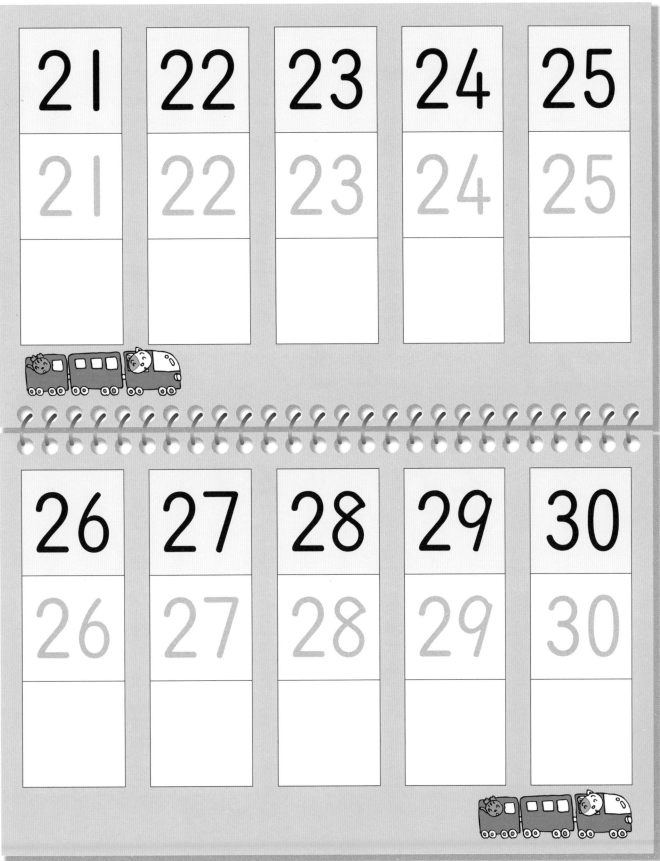

■Trace the gray numbers and fill in the missing numbers.
 Say each number aloud.

| 21 | 22 | 23 | 24 | 25 |
| 26 | 27 | 28 | 29 | 30 |

| 21 | | 23 | | 25 |
| | 27 | | 29 | |

| 21 | | | | |
| | | | | 30 |

12 Numbers 1 to 30

Name

Date

■ Fill in the missing numbers. Say each number aloud.

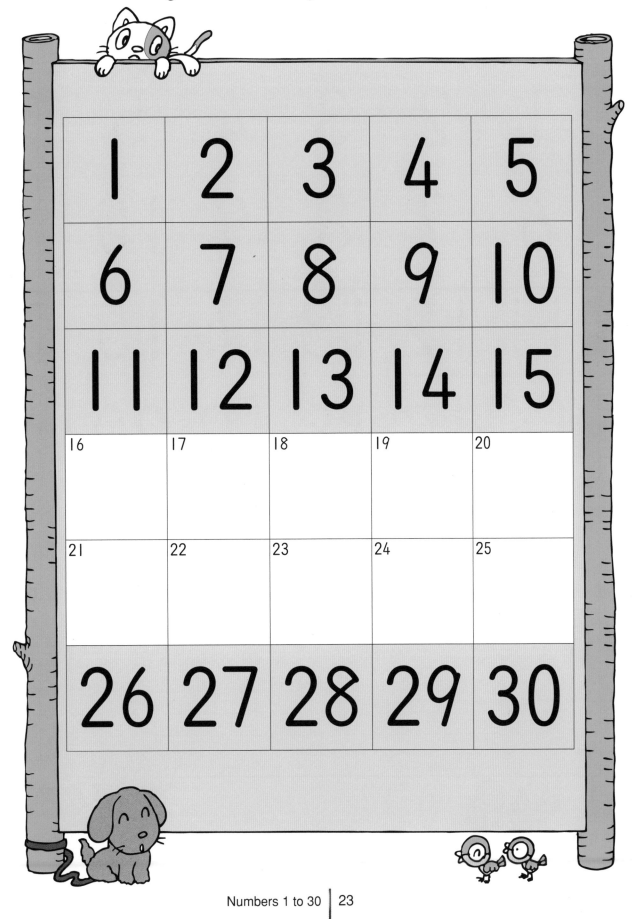

1	2	3	4	5
6	7	8	9	10
11	12	13	14	15
16	17	18	19	20
21	22	23	24	25
26	27	28	29	30

■Fill in the missing numbers. Say each number aloud.

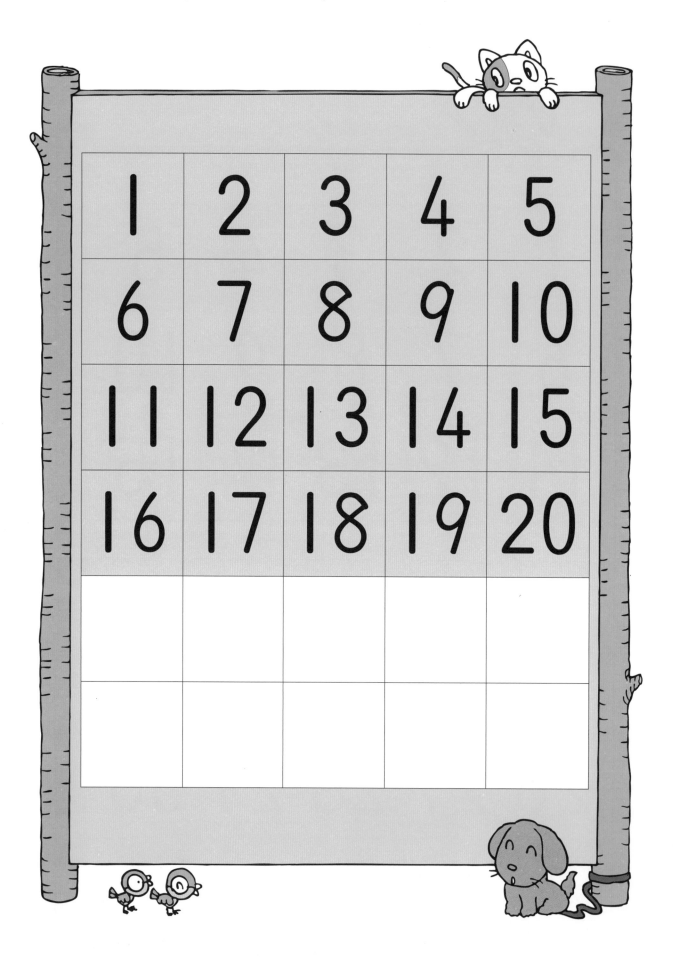

1	2	3	4	5
6	7	8	9	10
11	12	13	14	15
16	17	18	19	20

Numbers 1 to 30

To parents
Have your child write the 10 missing numbers in each group of 30.

Name

Date

■ Fill in the missing numbers. Say each number aloud.

1	2	3	4	5	6	7	8	9	10
11	12	13	14	15	16	17	18	19	20
21	22	23	24	25	26	27	28	29	30

1	2	3	4	5					
					16	17	18	19	20
21	22	23	24	25	26	27	28	29	30

Fill in the missing numbers. Say each number aloud.

1	2	3		5	6	7	8	9	10
21	22	23	24	25	26	27	28	29	30

1	2	3	4	5	6	7	8	9	10
11	12	13	14	15					
					26	27	28	29	30

Name

Date

To parents
Have your child use the table on this page to make it easier to count numbers from 31 to 50.

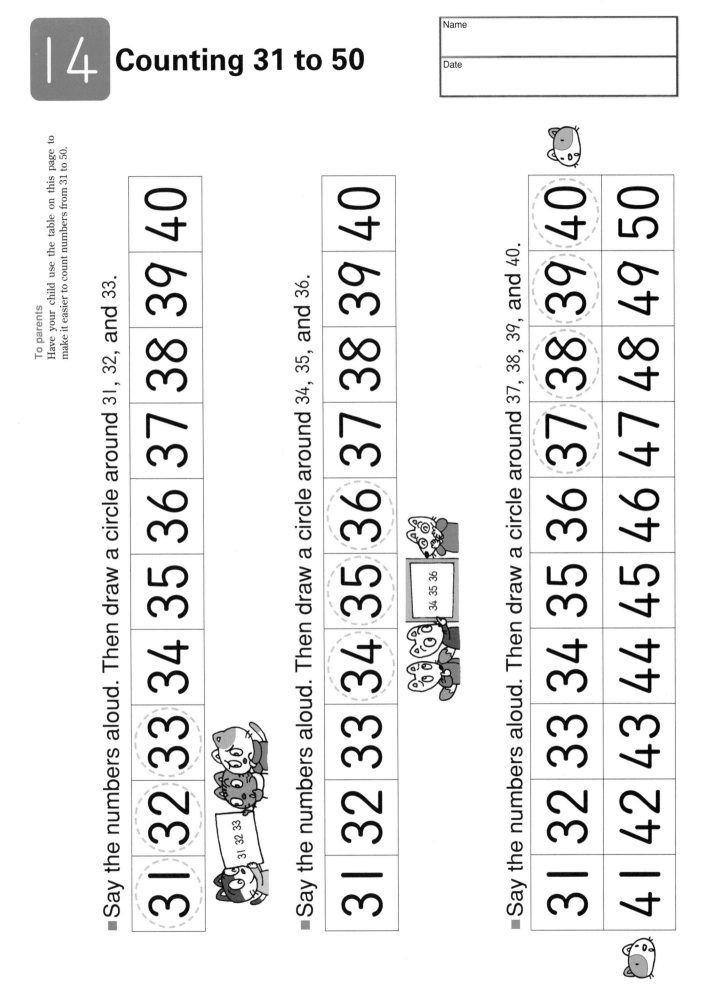

■ Say the numbers aloud. Then draw a circle around 31, 32, and 33.

| 31 | 32 | 33 | 34 | 35 | 36 | 37 | 38 | 39 | 40 |

■ Say the numbers aloud. Then draw a circle around 34, 35, and 36.

| 31 | 32 | 33 | 34 | 35 | 36 | 37 | 38 | 39 | 40 |

■ Say the numbers aloud. Then draw a circle around 37, 38, 39, and 40.

| 31 | 32 | 33 | 34 | 35 | 36 | 37 | 38 | 39 | 40 |
| 41 | 42 | 43 | 44 | 45 | 46 | 47 | 48 | 49 | 50 |

■ Say the numbers aloud. Then draw a circle around 41, 42, and 43.

31	32	33	34	35	36	37	38	39	40
(41)	(42)	(43)	44	45	46	47	48	49	50

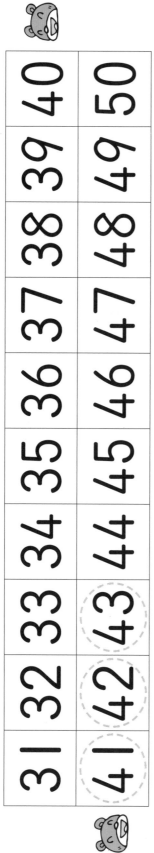

■ Say the numbers aloud. Then draw a circle around 44, 45, and 46.

41	42	43	44	45	46	47	48	49	50

44 45 46

■ Say the numbers aloud. Then draw a circle around 47, 48, 49, and 50.

41	42	43	44	45	46	47	48	49	50

47 48 49 50

Number Puzzle 1 to 40
Stuffed Animal

Name

Date

Draw a line from 21 to 40 in order while saying each number.

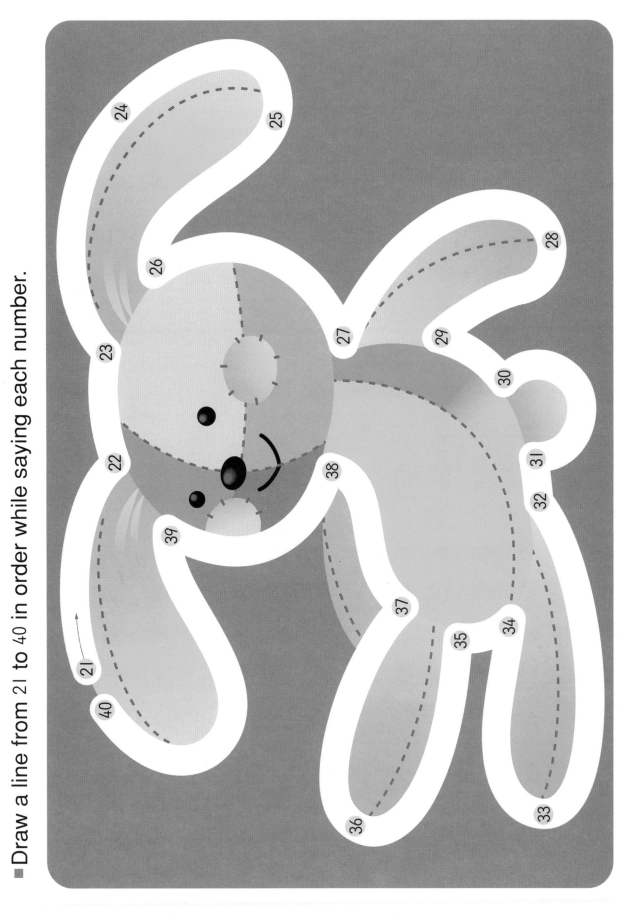

Who Is the Mouse's Friend?

■ Draw a line from 1 to 40 in order while saying each number.

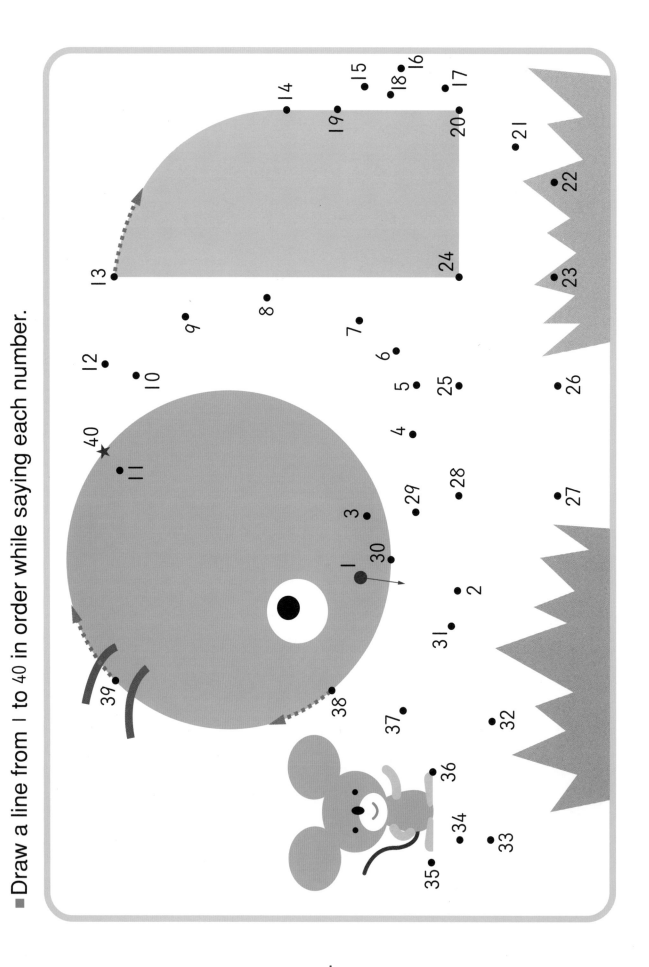

Number Puzzle 11 to 50
Bat

Name

Date

Draw a line from 31 to 50 in order while saying each number.

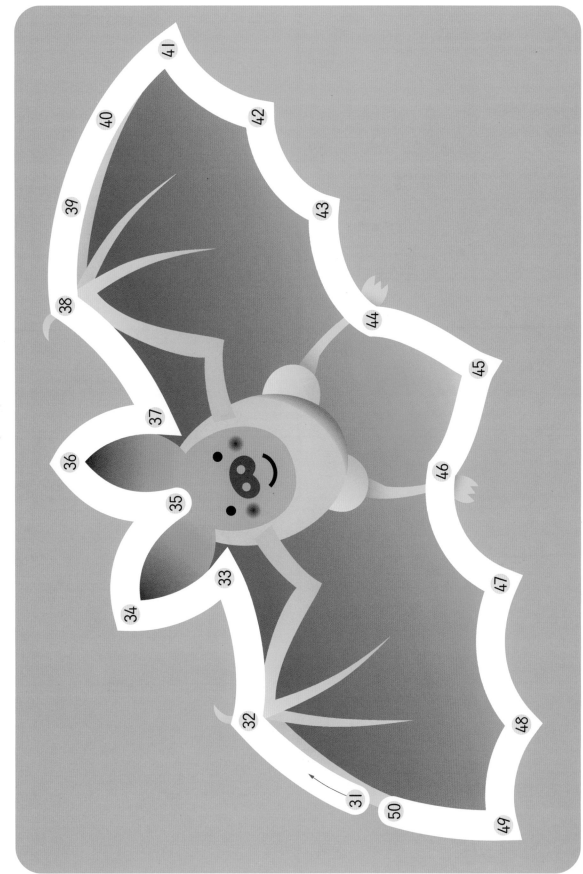

Who Is the Cat's Friend?

Draw a line from 11 to 50 in order while saying each number.

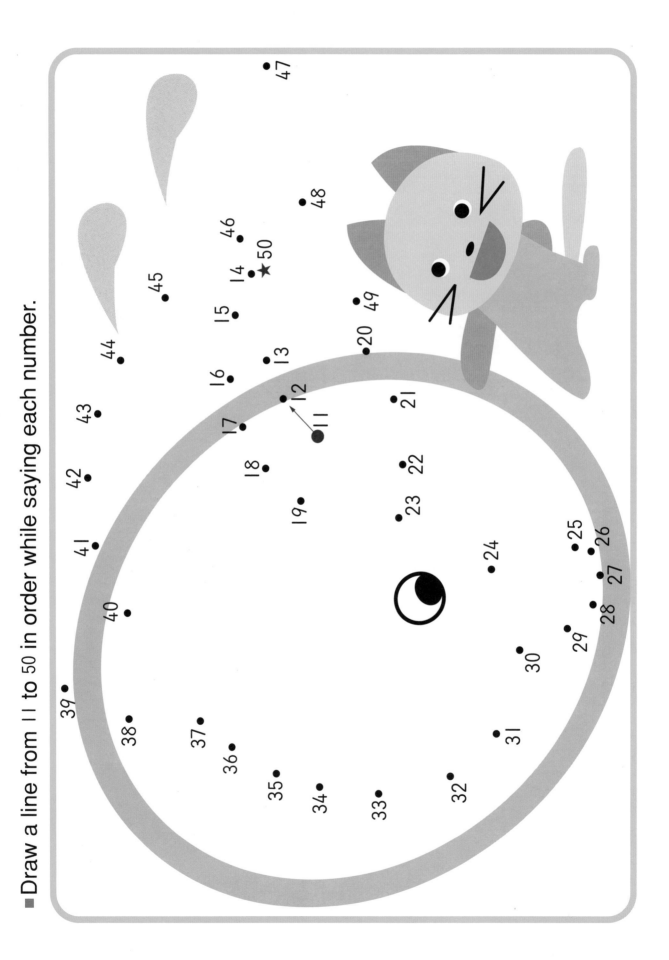

Numbers 21 to 50

Name

Date

Trace the gray numbers and fill in the missing numbers. Say each number aloud.

21	22	23	24	25	26	27	28	29	30
31	32	33	34	35	36	37	38	39	40

21	22	23	24	25	26	27	28	29	30
31	32	33	34	35	36	37	38	39	40

31	32	33	34	35	36	37	38	39	40
41	42	43	44	45	46	47	48	49	50

31	32	33	34	35	36	37	38	39	40
41	42	43	44	45	46	47	48	49	50

Writing Numbers 28 to 40

Name

Date

Trace the gray numbers and fill in the missing numbers. Say each number aloud.

(1)

(2)

| 26 | 27 | 28 | 29 | 30 | 31 | 32 | 33 | 34 | 35 | 36 | 37 | 38 | 39 | 40 |

■ Trace the gray numbers and fill in the missing numbers. Say each number aloud.

(1)

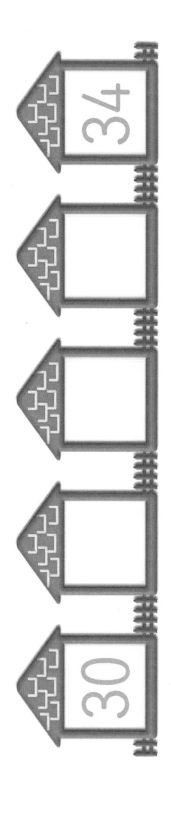

(2)

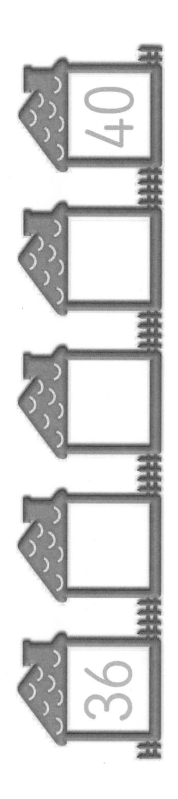

| 26 | 27 | 28 | 29 | 30 | 31 | 32 | 33 | 34 | 35 | 36 | 37 | 38 | 39 | 40 |

Name

Date

■Trace the gray numbers and fill in the missing numbers. Say each number aloud.

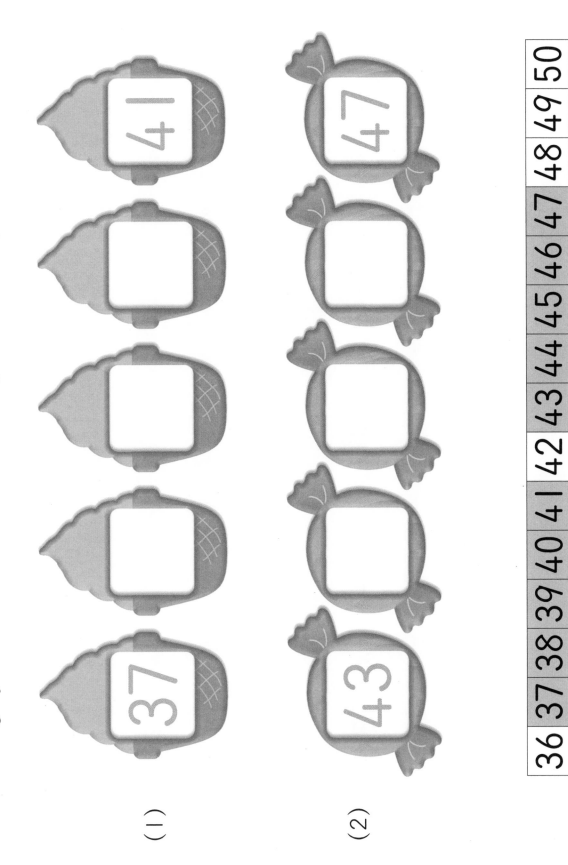

(1) 41   37

(2) 47   43

36	37	38	39	40	41	42	43	44	45	46	47	48	49	50

■Trace the gray numbers and fill in the missing numbers. Say each number aloud.

(1) 40 □ □ □ 44

(2) 46 □ □ □ 50

36	37	38	39	40	41	42	43	44	45	46	47	48	49	50

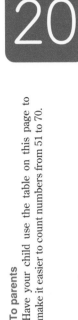

20 Counting 51 to 70

To parents
Have your child use the table on this page to make it easier to count numbers from 51 to 70.

Name

Date

■ Say the numbers aloud. Then draw a circle around 51, 52, and 53.

51	52	53	54	55	56	57	58	59	60

■ Say the numbers aloud. Then draw a circle around 54, 55, and 56.

51	52	53	54	55	56	57	58	59	60

■ Say the numbers aloud. Then draw a circle around 57, 58, 59, and 60.

51	52	53	54	55	56	57	58	59	60
61	62	63	64	65	66	67	68	69	70

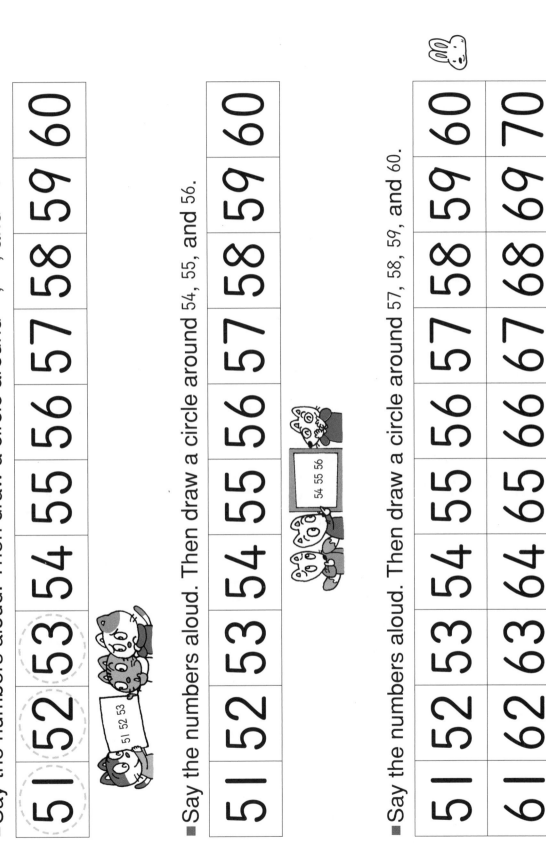

■ Say the numbers aloud. Then draw a circle around 61, 62, and 63.

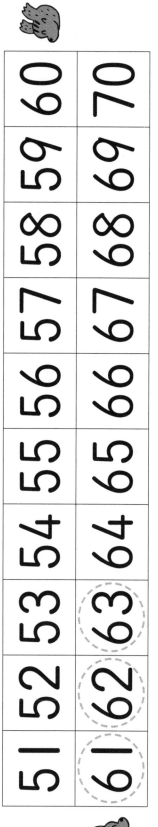

| 51 | 52 | 53 | 54 | 55 | 56 | 57 | 58 | 59 | 60 |
| 61 | 62 | 63 | 64 | 65 | 66 | 67 | 68 | 69 | 70 |

■ Say the numbers aloud. Then draw a circle around 64, 65, and 66.

| 61 | 62 | 63 | 64 | 65 | 66 | 67 | 68 | 69 | 70 |

64 65 66

■ Say the numbers aloud. Then draw a circle around 67, 68, 69, and 70.

| 61 | 62 | 63 | 64 | 65 | 66 | 67 | 68 | 69 | 70 |

67 68 69 70

Number Puzzle 11 to 60
Swordfish

Name

Date

Draw a line from 41 to 60 in order while saying each number.

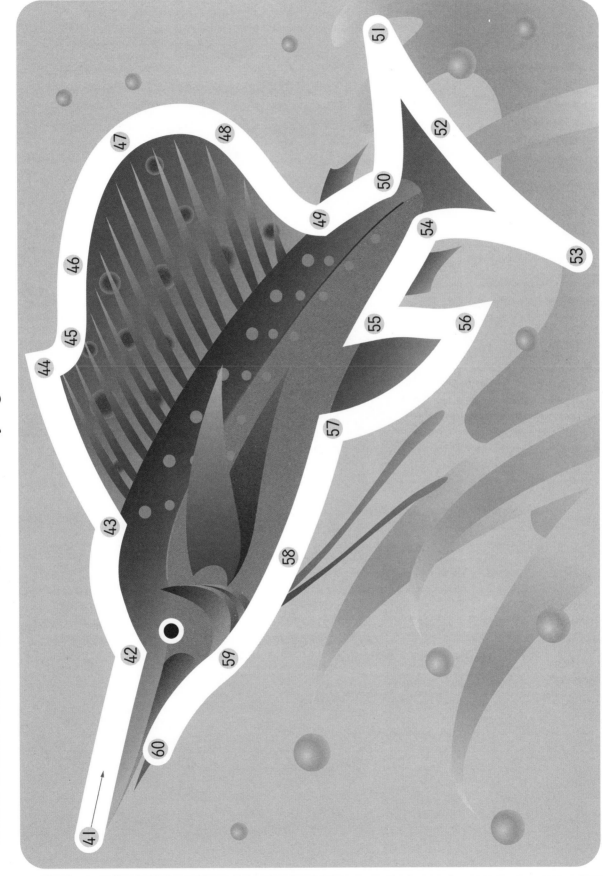

How Many Balloons?

Draw a line from 11 to 60 in order while saying each number.

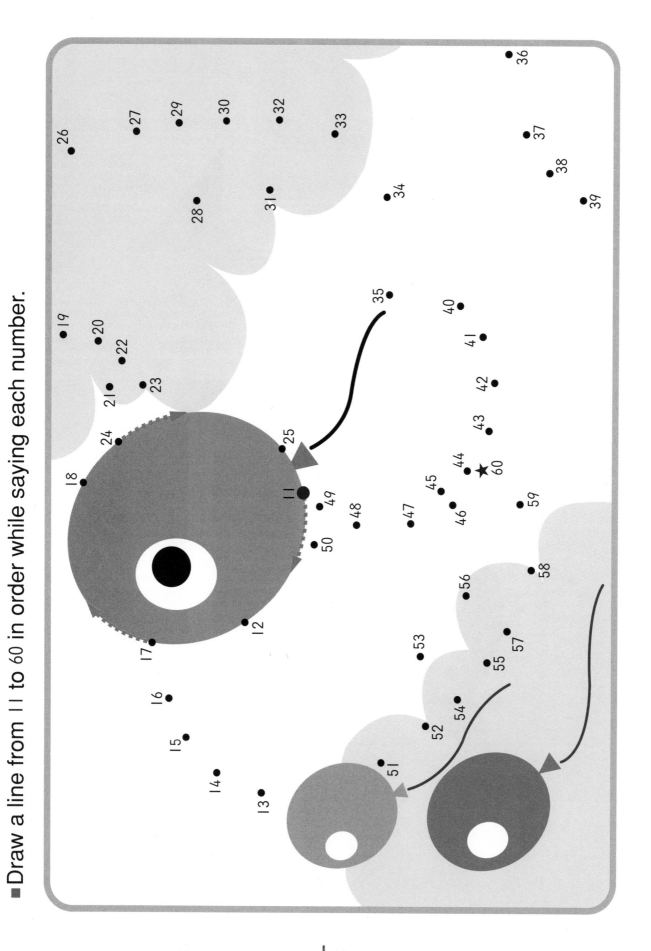

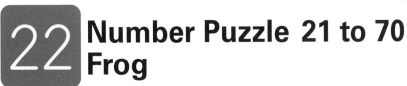

Name

Date

■Draw a line from 51 to 70 in order while saying each number.

Who Is Hiding in the Bushes?

Draw a line from 21 to 70 in order while saying each number.

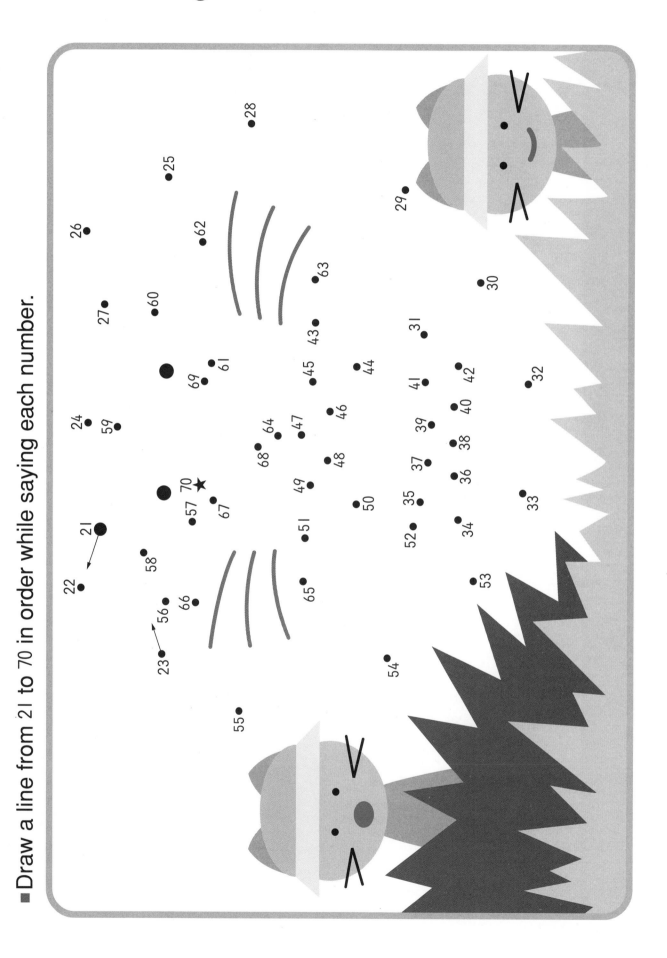

23 Numbers 41 to 70

Name

Date

■Trace the gray numbers and fill in the missing numbers. Say each number aloud.

| 41 | 42 | 43 | 44 | 45 | 46 | 47 | 48 | 49 | 50 |
| 51 | 52 | 53 | 54 | 55 | 56 | 57 | 58 | 59 | 60 |

| 41 | 42 | 43 | 44 | 45 | 46 | 47 | 48 | 49 | 50 |
| 51 | 52 | 53 | 54 | 55 | 56 | 57 | 58 | 59 | 60 |

■ Trace the gray numbers and fill in the missing numbers. Say each number aloud.

51	52	53	54	55	56	57	58	59	60
61	62	63	64	65	66	67	68	69	70

51	52	53	54	55	56	57	58	59	60
61	62	63	64	65	66	67	68	69	70

Name

Date

■Trace the gray numbers and fill in the missing numbers. Say each number aloud.

(1)

47 48 49 50 51

(2)

53   57

46 47 48 49 50 51 52 53 54 55 56 57 58 59 60

■Trace the gray numbers and fill in the missing numbers. Say each number aloud.

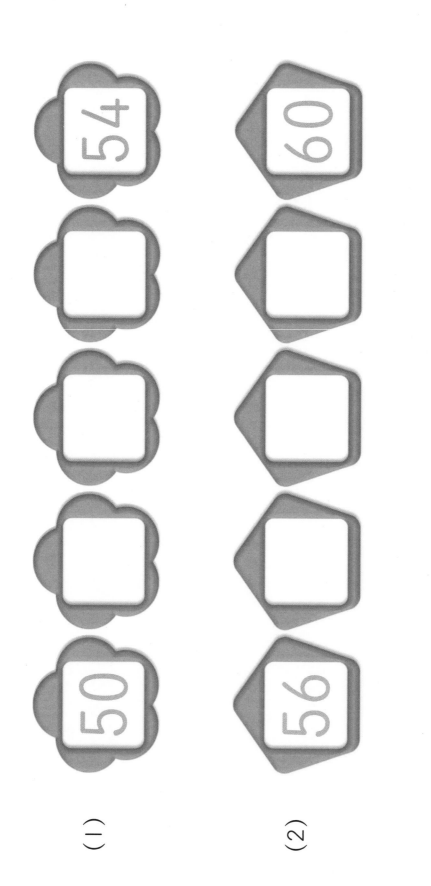

(1) 50 □ □ □ 54

(2) 56 □ □ □ 60

46 47 48 49 50 51 52 53 54 55 56 57 58 59 60

25 Writing Numbers 58 to 70

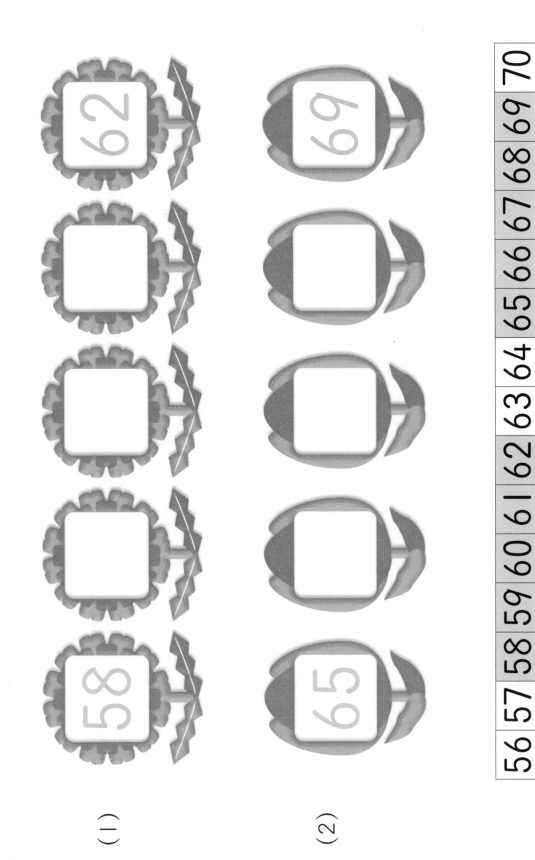

Name

Date

■Trace the gray numbers and fill in the missing numbers. Say each number aloud.

(1) 58 □ □ □ 62

(2) 65 □ □ □ 69

56 57 58 59 60 61 62 63 64 65 66 67 68 69 70

■ Trace the gray numbers and fill in the missing numbers. Say each number aloud.

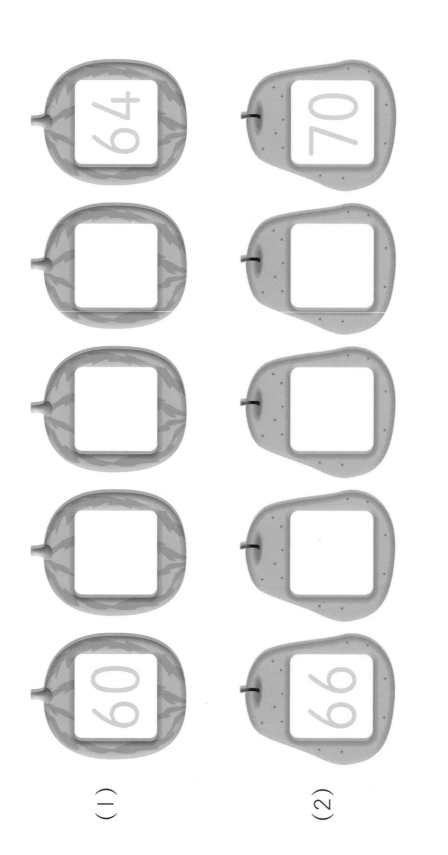

(1) 60 □ □ □ 64

(2) 66 □ □ □ 70

| 56 | 57 | 58 | 59 | 60 | 61 | 62 | 63 | 64 | 65 | 66 | 67 | 68 | 69 | 70 |

Name

Date

■ Say the numbers aloud. Then draw a circle around 71, 72, and 73.

| 71 | 72 | 73 | 74 | 75 | 76 | 77 | 78 | 79 | 80 |

71 72 73

■ Say the numbers aloud. Then draw a circle around 74, 75, and 76.

| 71 | 72 | 73 | 74 | 75 | 76 | 77 | 78 | 79 | 80 |

74 75 76

■ Say the numbers aloud. Then draw a circle around 77, 78, 79, and 80.

| 71 | 72 | 73 | 74 | 75 | 76 | 77 | 78 | 79 | 80 |
| 81 | 82 | 83 | 84 | 85 | 86 | 87 | 88 | 89 | 90 |

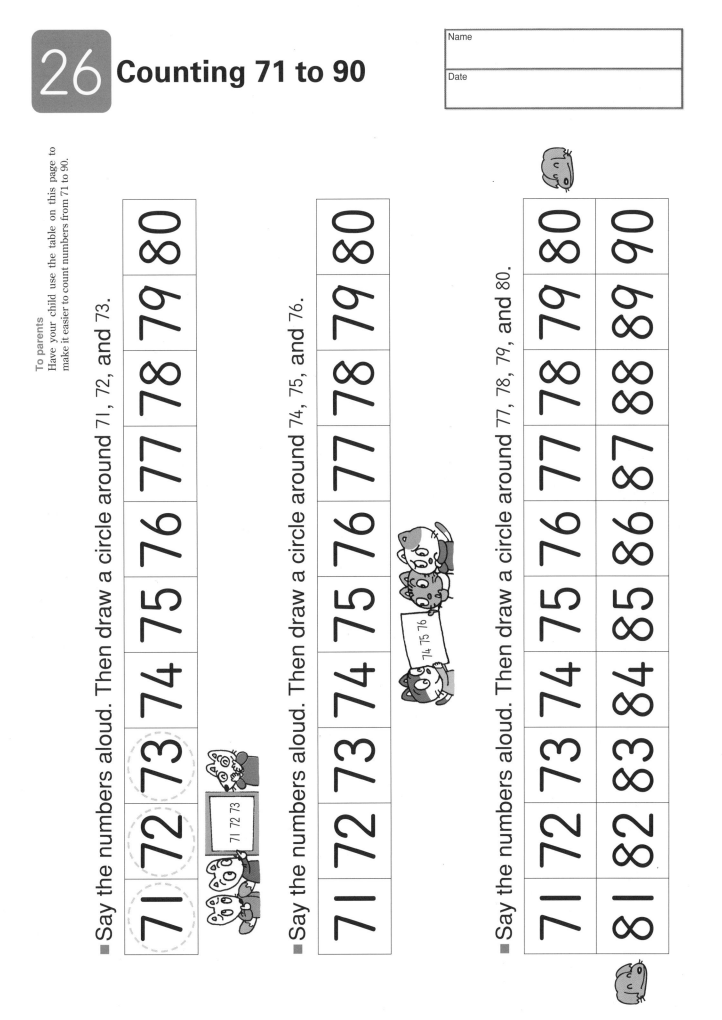

■ Say the numbers aloud. Then draw a circle around 81, 82, and 83.

| 71 | 72 | 73 | 74 | 75 | 76 | 77 | 78 | 79 | 80 |
| (81) | (82) | (83) | 84 | 85 | 86 | 87 | 88 | 89 | 90 |

■ Say the numbers aloud. Then draw a circle around 84, 85, and 86.

| 81 | 82 | 83 | 84 | 85 | 86 | 87 | 88 | 89 | 90 |

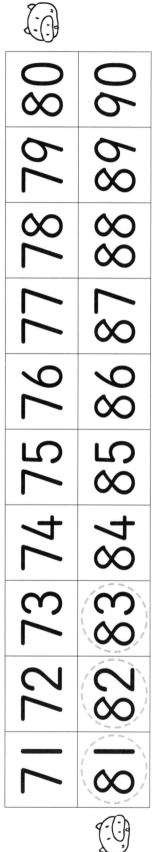

84 85 86

■ Say the numbers aloud. Then draw a circle around 87, 88, 89, and 90.

| 81 | 82 | 83 | 84 | 85 | 86 | 87 | 88 | 89 | 90 |

87 88 89 90

Name

Date

Draw a line from 61 to 80 in order while saying each number.

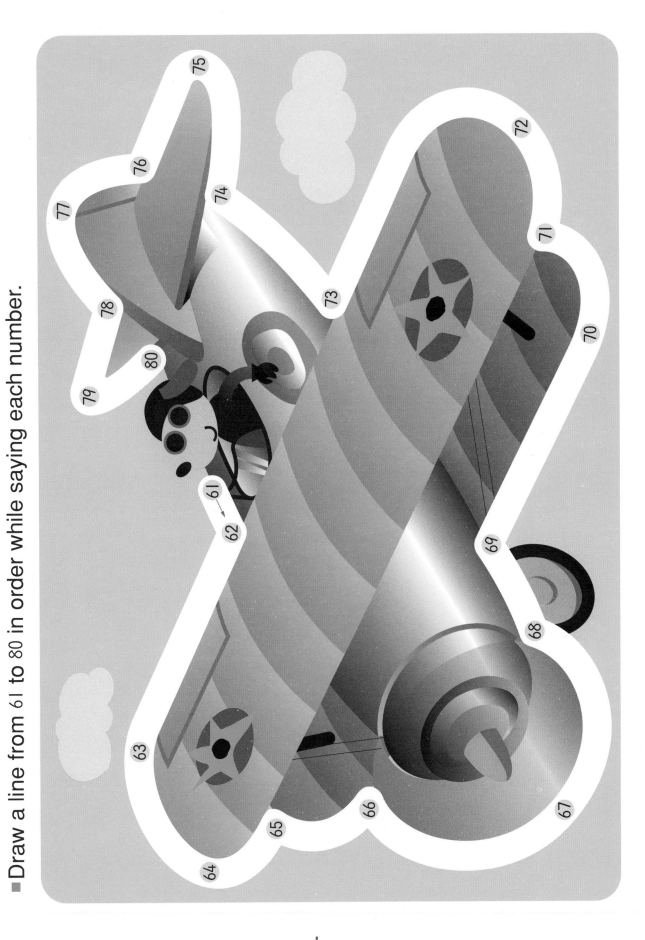

What's Under the Sea?

Draw a line from 31 to 80 in order while saying each number.

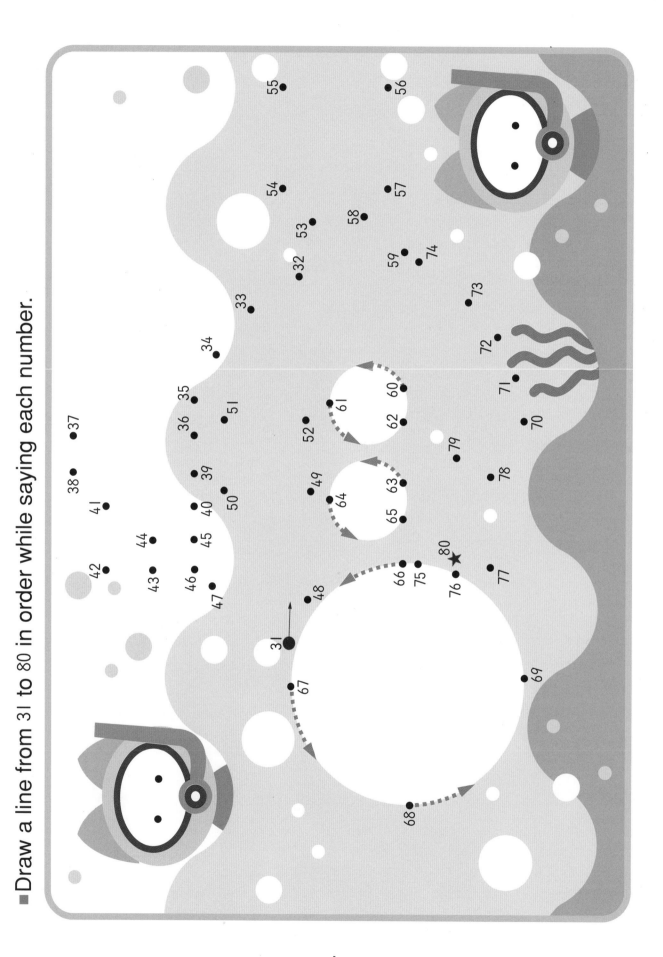

Name

Date

■ Draw a line from 71 to 90 in order while saying each number.

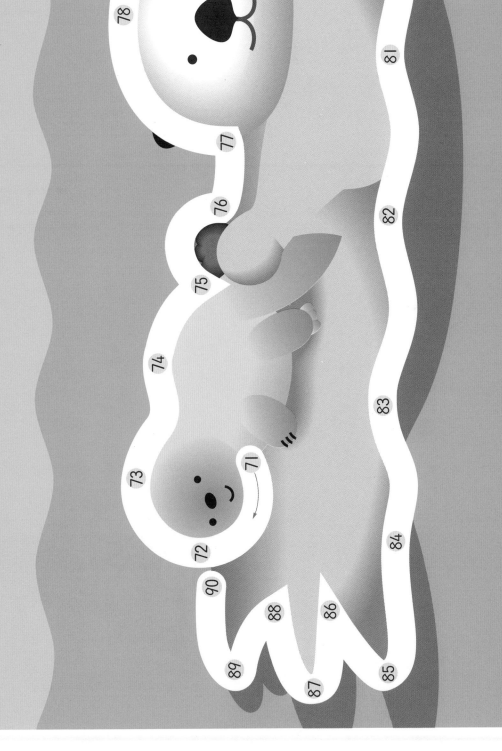

I'm Going to Eat You!

Draw a line from 41 to 90 in order while saying each number.

Numbers 61 to 90

Name

Date

Trace the gray numbers and fill in the missing numbers. Say each number aloud.

First chart:

61	62	63	64	65	66	67	68	69	70
71	72	73	74	75	76	77	78	79	80

Second chart:

61	62	63	64	65	66	67	68	69	70
71	72	73	74	75	76	77	78	79	80

■Trace the gray numbers and fill in the missing numbers. Say each number aloud.

71	72	73	74	75	76	77	78	79	80
81	82	83	84	85	86	87	88	89	90

71	72	73	74	75	76	77	78	79	80
81	82	83	84	85	86	87	88	89	90

■Trace the gray numbers and fill in the missing numbers. Say each number aloud.

(1)

67 68 69 70 71

(2)

74　　　　78

66 67 68 69 70 71 72 73 74 75 76 77 78 79 80

■Trace the gray numbers and fill in the missing numbers. Say each number aloud.

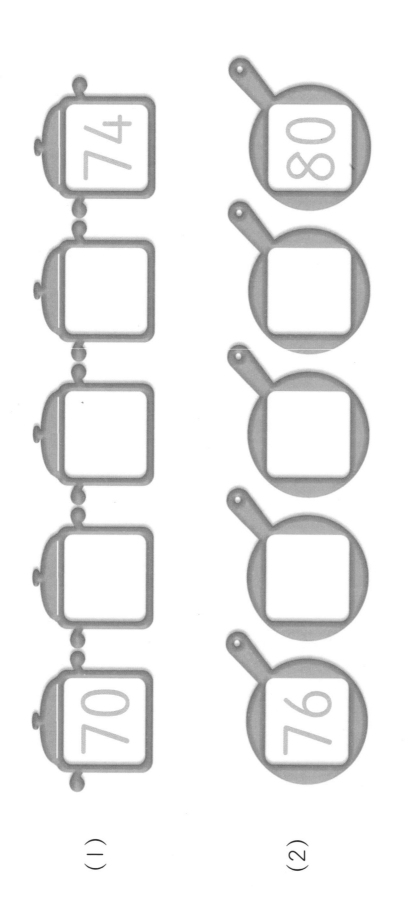

(1)

70 ___ ___ 74

(2)

76 ___ ___ 80

66 67 68 69 70 71 72 73 74 75 76 77 78 79 80

■ Trace the gray numbers and fill in the missing numbers. Say each number aloud.

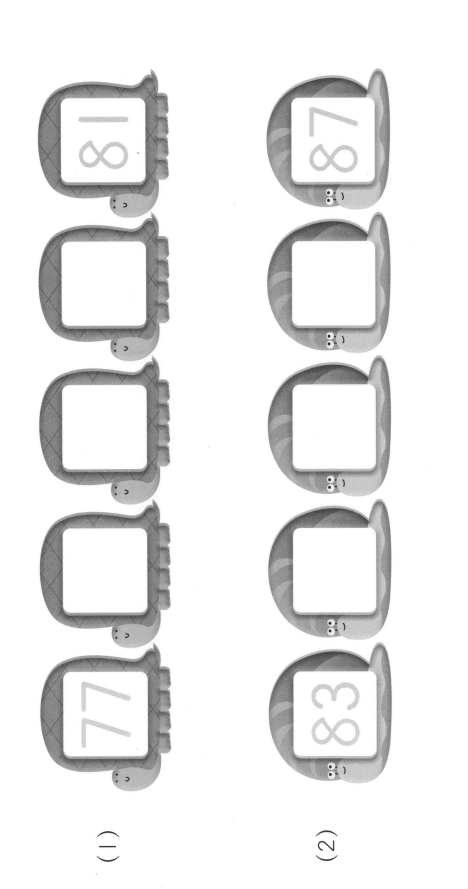

(1) 77 [ ] [ ] [ ] 81

(2) 83 [ ] [ ] [ ] 87

76 77 78 79 80 81 82 83 84 85 86 87 88 89 90

■Trace the gray numbers and fill in the missing numbers. Say each number aloud.

(1)

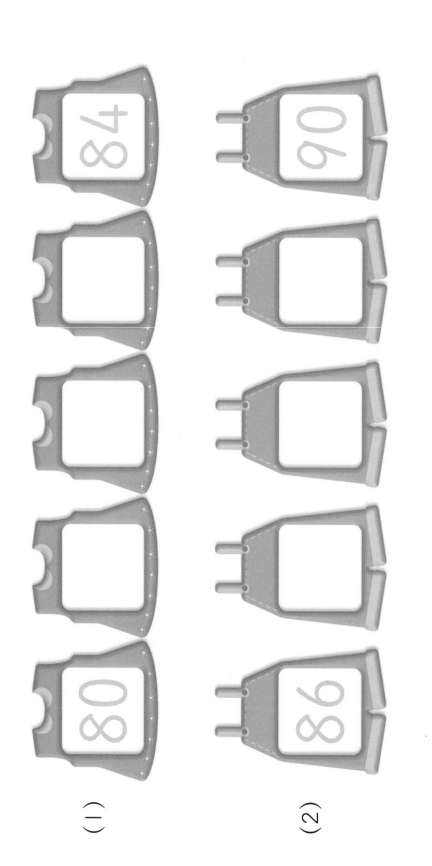

80   84

(2)

86   90

76 77 78 79 80 81 82 83 84 85 86 87 88 89 90

Counting 91 to 110

Name

Date

To parents
Have your child use the table on pages 63, 64, and 67 to make it easier to count numbers from 91 to 120.

■ Say the numbers aloud. Then draw a circle around 91, 92, and 93.

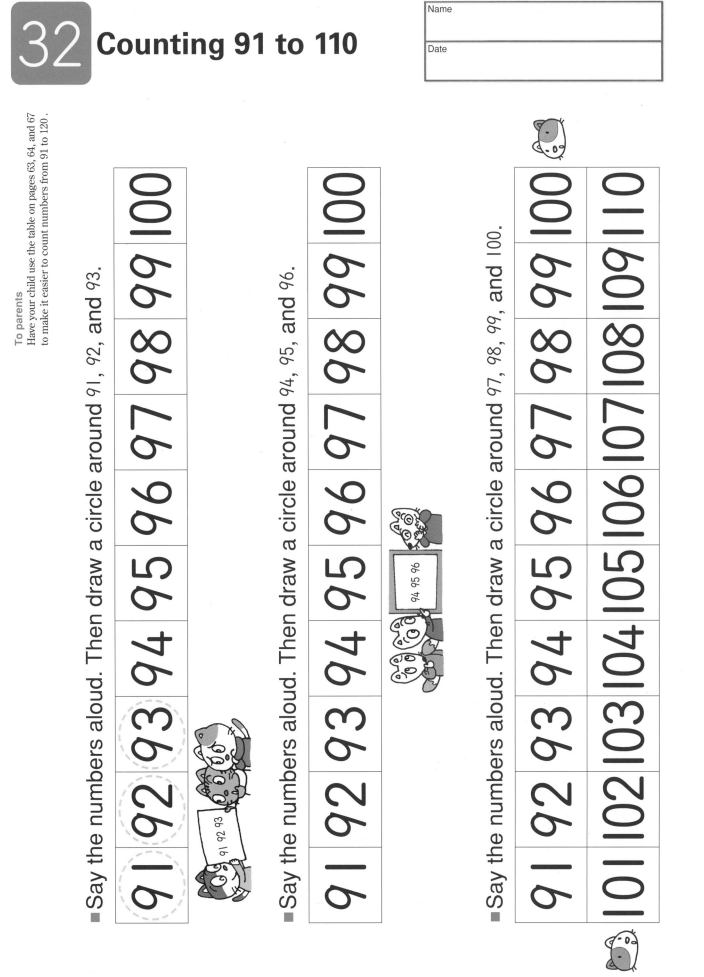

| 91 | 92 | 93 | 94 | 95 | 96 | 97 | 98 | 99 | 100 |

■ Say the numbers aloud. Then draw a circle around 94, 95, and 96.

| 91 | 92 | 93 | 94 | 95 | 96 | 97 | 98 | 99 | 100 |

■ Say the numbers aloud. Then draw a circle around 97, 98, 99, and 100.

| 91 | 92 | 93 | 94 | 95 | 96 | 97 | 98 | 99 | 100 |
| 101 | 102 | 103 | 104 | 105 | 106 | 107 | 108 | 109 | 110 |

■ Say the numbers aloud. Then draw a circle around 101, 102, and 103.

91	92	93	94	95	96	97	98	99	100
(101)	(102)	(103)	104	105	106	107	108	109	110

■ Say the numbers aloud. Then draw a circle around 104, 105, and 106.

101	102	103	104	105	106	107	108	109	110

■ Say the numbers aloud. Then draw a circle around 107, 108, 109, and 110.

101	102	103	104	105	106	107	108	109	110

Draw a line from 71 to 100 in order while saying each number.

Cat in Space

■ Draw a line from 51 to 100 in order while saying each number.

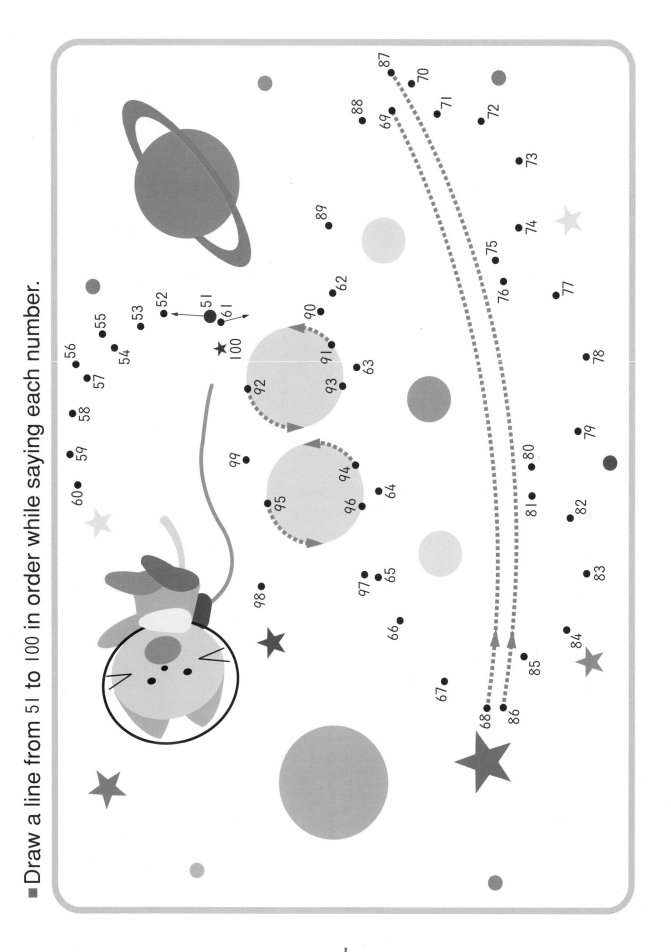

34 Numbers 91 to 120

Name

Date

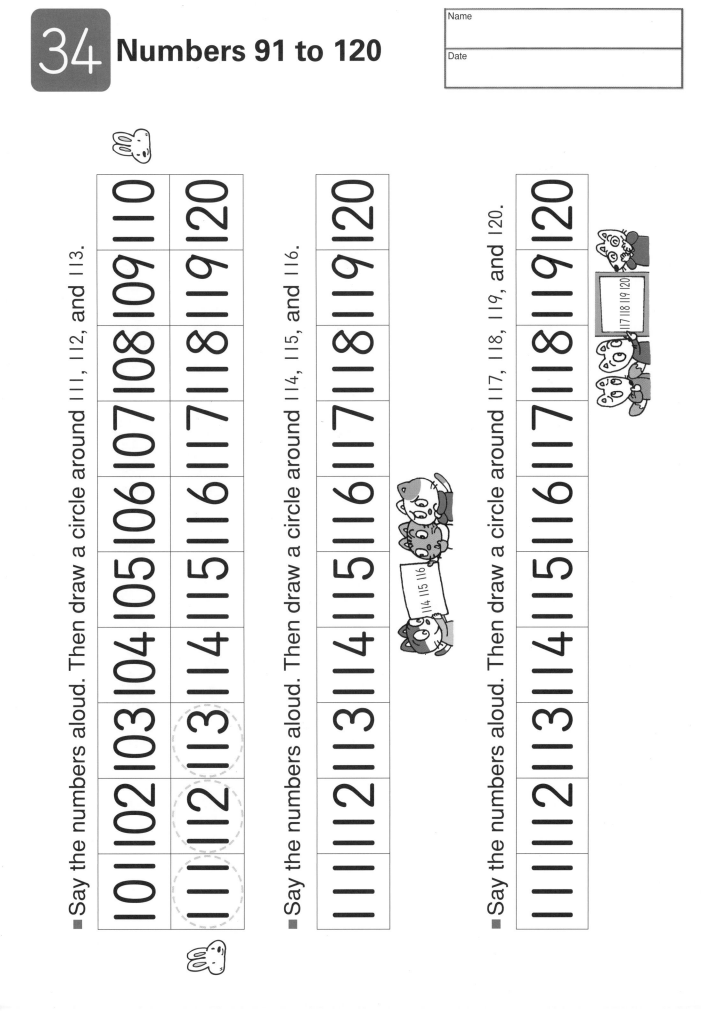

■ Say the numbers aloud. Then draw a circle around 111, 112, and 113.

| 101 | 102 | 103 | 104 | 105 | 106 | 107 | 108 | 109 | 110 |
| 111 | 112 | 113 | 114 | 115 | 116 | 117 | 118 | 119 | 120 |

■ Say the numbers aloud. Then draw a circle around 114, 115, and 116.

| 111 | 112 | 113 | 114 | 115 | 116 | 117 | 118 | 119 | 120 |

■ Say the numbers aloud. Then draw a circle around 117, 118, 119, and 120.

| 111 | 112 | 113 | 114 | 115 | 116 | 117 | 118 | 119 | 120 |

Sailing Ship

Draw a line from 91 to 120 in order while saying each number.

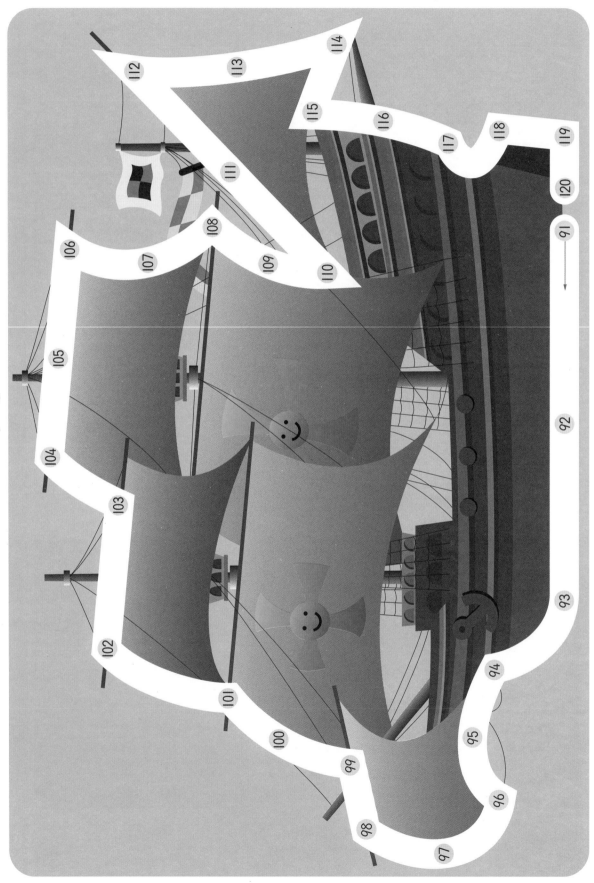

Numbers 71 to 120
Helicopter

Name

Date

■ Draw a line from 71 to 120 in order while saying each number.

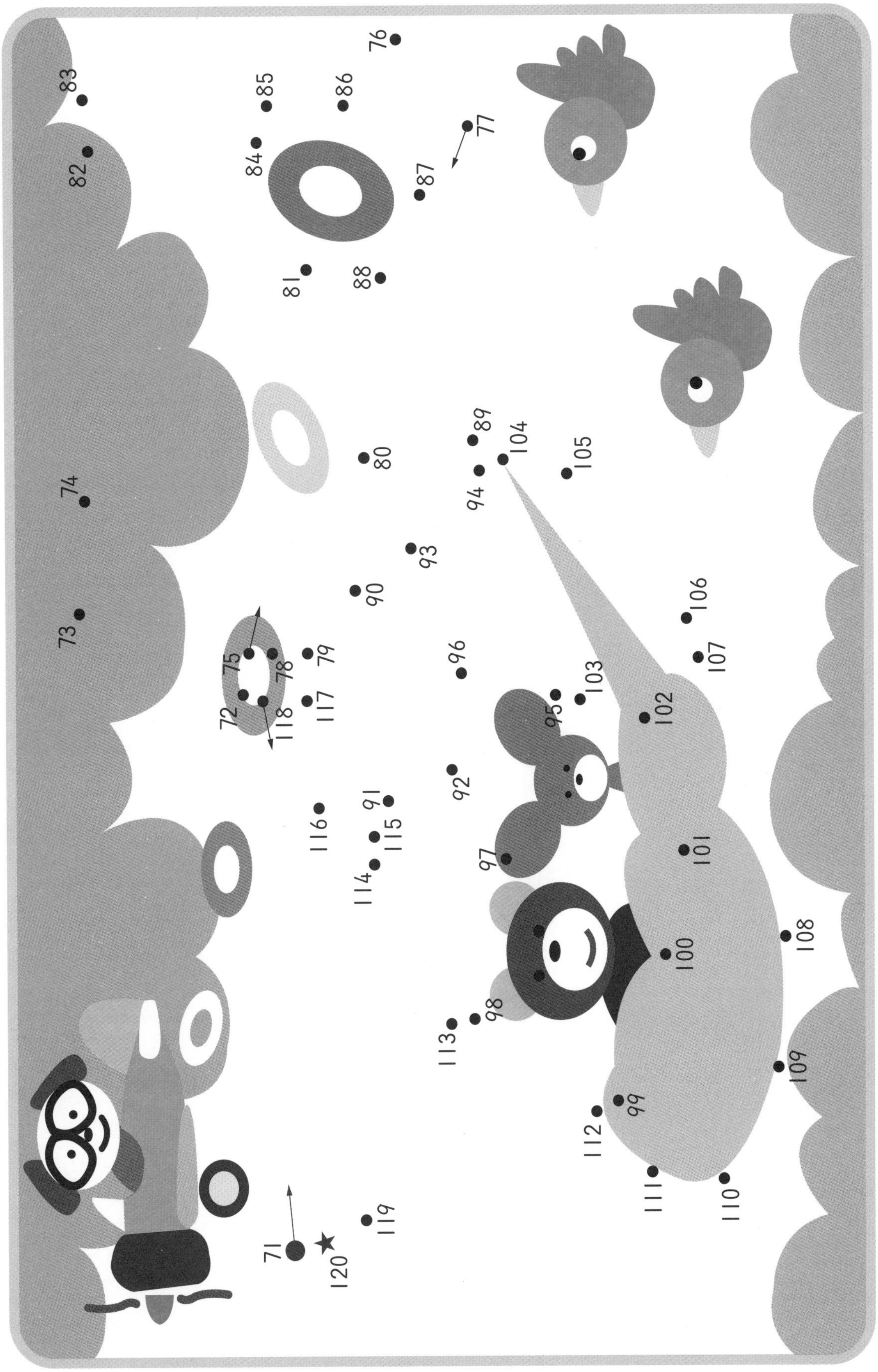

76
83
85
86
82
84
77
87
81
88
74
80
73
93
75 79
90
78
72 117
118
96
116 91
92
115
103
114
95
97
101
113
98
100
108
112
109
99
111
110
71
120
119

104
89
94
105
106
107
102

Trace the gray numbers and fill in the missing numbers. Say each number aloud.

81	82	83	84	85	86	87	88	89	90
91	92	93	94	95	96	97	98	99	100
101	102	103	104	105	106	107	108	109	110

91	92	93	94	95	96	97	98	99	100
101	102	103	104	105	106	107	108	109	110
111	112	113	114	115	116	117	118	119	120

36 **Numbers 87 to 120**

Name

Date

■ Trace the gray numbers and fill in the missing numbers. Say each number aloud.

91	92	93	94	95	96	97	98	99	100
101	102	103	104	105	106	107	108	109	110
111	112	113	114	115	116	117	118	119	120

91	92	93	94	95	96	97	98	99	100
101	102	103	104	105	106	107	108	109	110
111	112	113	114	115	116	117	118	119	120

■Trace the gray numbers and fill in the missing numbers. Say each number aloud.

(1) 87 88 89 90 91

(2) 95 □ □ □ 96

| 86 | 87 | 88 | 89 | 90 | 91 | 92 | 93 | 94 | 95 | 96 | 97 | 98 | 99 | 100 |

37 Writing Numbers 90 to 108

Name

Date

■Trace the gray numbers and fill in the missing numbers. Say each number aloud.

(1)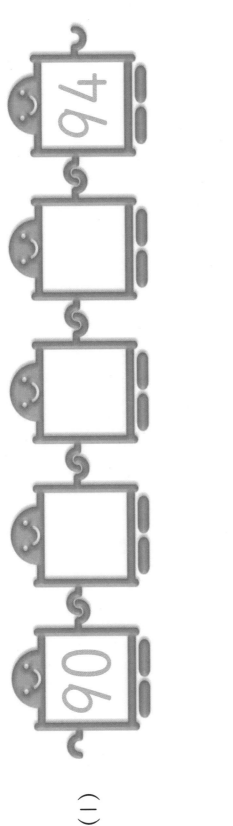

(2)

86 87 88 89 90 91 92 93 94 95 96 97 98 99 100

■ Trace the gray numbers and fill in the missing numbers. Say each number aloud.

(1)

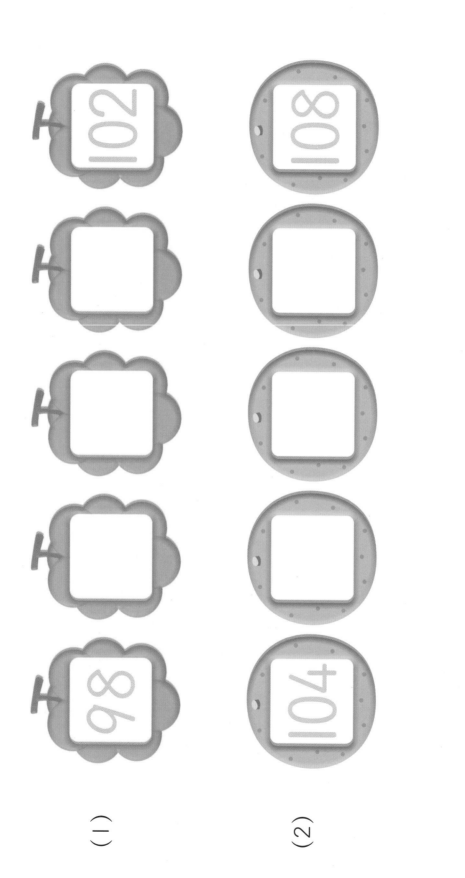

96

102

(2)

104

108

| 96 | 97 | 98 | 99 | 100 | 101 | 102 | 103 | 104 | 105 | 106 | 107 | 108 | 109 | 110 |

38 Writing Numbers 102 to 120

■ Trace the gray numbers and fill in the missing numbers. Say each number aloud.

(1)

(2)

101 | 102 | 103 | 104 | 105 | 106 | 107 | 108 | 109 | 110 | 111 | 112 | 113 | 114 | 115

■ Trace the gray numbers and fill in the missing numbers. Say each number aloud.

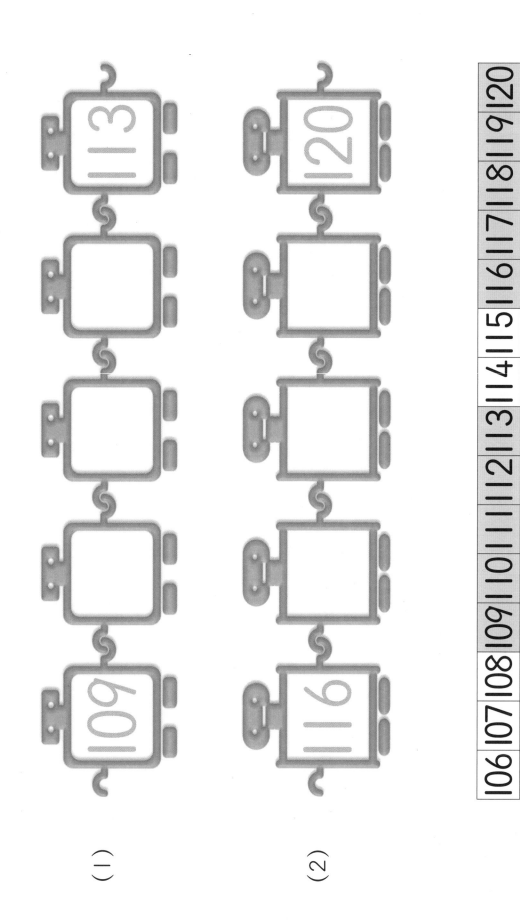

(1) 109 ___ ___ ___ 113

(2) 116 ___ ___ ___ 120

106 107 108 109 110 111 112 113 114 115 116 117 118 119 120

Name

Date

To parents
From this page to the end, there are exercises to write numbers from 1 to 120. Small-sized numbers are included as hints.

■ Fill in the missing numbers. Say each number aloud.

1	2	3 4	5 6	7 8	9 10
11 12	13 14	15 16	17 18	19 20
21 22	23 24	25 26	27 28	29 30
31 32	33 34	35 36	37 38	39 40
41 42	43 44	45 46	47 48	49 50
51 52	53 54	55 56	57 58	59 60

Fill in the missing numbers. Say each number aloud.

62		64		66		68		70
72		74		76		78		80
82		84		86		88		90
92		94		96		98		100
102		104		106		108		110
112		114		116		118		120

40 Review 1 to 120

Name

Date

■Write the numbers in order from 31. Say each number aloud.

					60
1	2	3	4	5	6	7	8	9	10			
11	12	13	14	15	16	17	18	19	20			
21	22	23	24	25	26	27	28	29	30			

■Write the numbers in order from 61. Say each number aloud.

61									
									120

You are now able to count and write up to 120. Congratulations!

Certificate of Achievement

_____

is hereby congratulated on completing

My Book of Numbers 1 - 120

Presented on _____ , 20____

_____
Parent or Guardian